A LITTLE BEHIND

Christopher Moller

TO GEOFF AND GLADYS AND THE WOODPECKER FOR THE START

Published by Christopher Moller
Hammer Trout Farm
Liphook, Hants GU30 7JB

ISBN 0 9509125 1 4

Printed by Seven Corners Press Limited
Guildford, Surrey

CONTRARY TO POPULAR PRESS REPORTS OF THE GLORIOUS 12TH. AUGUST, THE MOORS DON'T ECHO TO THE 'CRACK' OF RIFLES

LIKE THE O.K. CORALL,

BUT TO THE MORE MELLOW SOUND OF THE SHOTGUN

THE WEAPON OF THE DISCERNING SPORTSMAN.

FOR GAME SHOOTING THIS ITEM MAY BE CONSIDERED ESSENTIAL, AND MAY BE OBTAINED FROM A GUNSMITH,

OR PERHAPS EVEN FROM OTHER SOURCES.

ALTHOUGH SHOTGUNS CAN BE OBTAINED FOR AS LITTLE,

. . . AS ONE HUNDRED POUNDS,

THEY CAN COST MANY THOUSANDS.

WHILST, IN DRIVEN SHOOTING, YOU WILL SEE AN INCREASING NUMBER OF 'OVER AND UNDERS'

THE MOST COMMON SIGHTS ARE

'SIDE-BY-SIDES'.

REPEATERS,

AND AUTOMATICS, ARE FROWNED UPON .

THE GAUGE, OR SIZE, OF SHOTGUNS RANGE FROM FOUR-TEN AND TWENTY EIGHT BORES,

USED BY BEGINNERS,

THROUGH TWENTY AND SIXTEEN BORES

FAVOURED BY THE LADIES,

THE OLDER MAN ,

AND SOME EXPERTS ;

TO THE TWELVE BORE

WHICH IS THE MOST WIDELY SEEN ;

AND FINALLY TO THE TEN AND EIGHT BORES

USED BY WILDFOWLERS FOR LARGER QUARRY.

HAVING CHOSEN YOUR WEAPON YOU MUST NOW BECOME FAMILIAR WITH ITS VARIOUS PARTS,

LIKE THE STOCK,

AND THE BARRELS;

THE BUTT

AND THE TRIGGER

AND THE FORE END.

TO LEARN TO SHOOT WITH YOUR NEW ACQUISITION, A SHOOTING SCHOOL IS TO BE RECOMMENDED.

THE MOST IMPORTANT MAN IS YOUR INSTRUCTOR,

WHO WILL SHOW YOU ROUND

THE VARIOUS FEATURES OF THE SCHOOL

AND INTRODUCE YOU TO YOUR TRAPPER

HE WILL EMPHASIZE THE IMPORTANCE
OF DISCIPLINE ,

AND SAFETY .

... AND OF COURSE WE RESERVE
THE RIGHT TO SHOOT BACK .

HE WILL SHOW YOU BASIC GUN-HANDLING

... AND GIVE YOU YOUR FIRST SIGHT OF

A CLAY PIGEON ,

THE TARGET WHICH CAN SIMULATE EVERYTHING

FROM THE CROSSING PIGEON,

THE SPRINGING TEAL ,

TO THE HIGH PHEASANT.

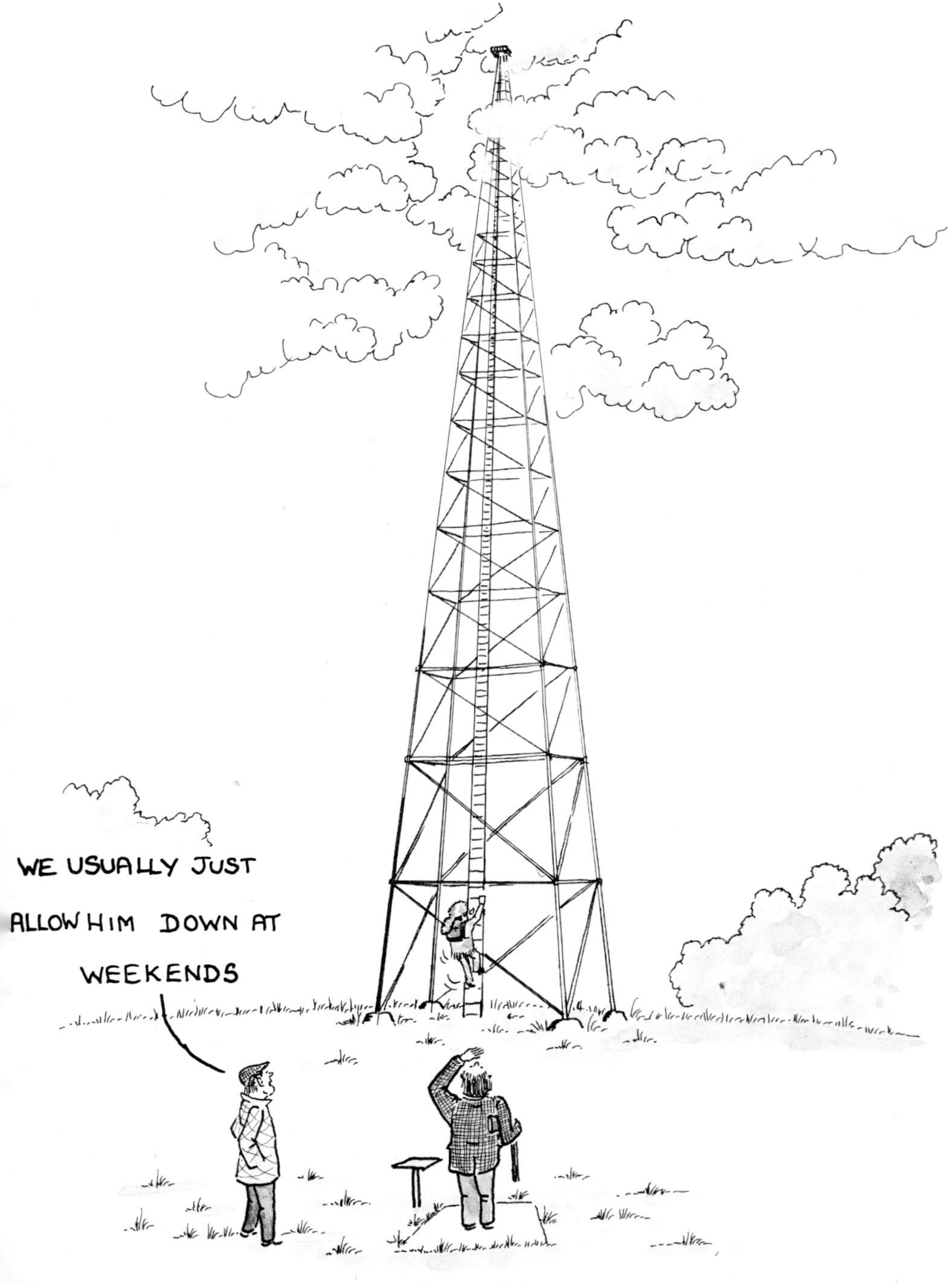

HE WILL MONITOR YOUR PROGRESS,

AND ADVISE ON YOUR MISTAKES.

BUT WITH PERSEVERANCE

YOU WILL GROW IN CONFIDENCE

UNTIL YOU ARE READY ,

– FINANCES ALLOWING ,

TO CONSIDER THE NEXT STAGE .

IT IS IMPORTANT TO HAVE A REASONABLE UNDERSTANDING

. . . OF THE LANGUAGE .

THE 'GUN' ALSO REFERS TO THE MAN POINTING THE WEAPON AT THE SKY, HOPING THAT THE

SHOT WILL COINCIDE WITH THE ARRIVAL OF A BIRD ;

THE 'HEADING' WHICH IS OTHERWISE KNOWN AS

THE 'FLUSHING POINT',

WHERE THE BIRDS ARE DRIVEN TO

BEFORE FLYING OVER THE GUNS ;

SHOOTING STICK – WHICH IS NOT RECOMMENDED

FOR TYING YOUR DOG TO

AS IT CAN BE DANGEROUS;

AND PEGS

WHERE YOU WILL WAIT FOR THE BIRDS TO BE DRIVEN OVER .

YOU MUST ALSO BECOME FAMILIAR WITH SUCH TERMS
AS SEWELLING ,

—A STRATEGICALLY PLACED BARRIER
WHICH PREVENTS ESCAPE—

TIPS,

GIVE THE COLONEL
A HAND, SOMEONE . . .

PRIVATE
&
GAME PRESERVE
KEEP OUT

THE BAG,

AND HEART-STARTERS ,

I'M AFRAID WE'VE GOT A BIT
OF A WALK TO THE NEXT ONE . . .

WHICH ARE CONCOCTED TO VARYING RECIPES,

SOME OLD,

AND SOME NEW.

DANGER
KEEP OUT
DON'T YOU THINK DEAR,
ITS TIME WE FOUND ANOTHER
PLACE TO PICK SLOES ?

SOME IMPORTANT ACQUISITIONS MAY BE MADE AT THIS STAGE, SUCH AS A VEHICLE

WHICH CAN CARRY PEOPLE AND EQUIPMENT.

A 'FOUR-WHEEL DRIVE' IS AN ADVANTAGE

FOR ITS ABILITY TO GO ALMOST ANYWHERE ...

THEY ARE NOT COMPULSORY HOWEVER ,

IF YOU HAVE ANYTHING IN PARTICULAR AGAINST THEM .

A SHOOTING DOG IS ANOTHER ACQUISITION

THAT CAN AFFECT YOUR STANDING WITH YOUR FELLOW GUNS

WHETHER IT BE THE SPRINGER SPANIEL ,

THE POINTER ,

THE IRISH SETTER ,

THE FLATCOAT,

AND THE EVER-POPULAR LABRADOR

WHICH ORIGINATED AS A WATER-RETRIEVER.

YOU MUST ALSO GET TO KNOW THE PROFESSIONALS

SUCH AS THE KEEPER , BLESS HIM .

THE GOOD KEEPER CAN COMMAND RESPECT

AT ALL TIMES ,

AND IT IS WISE TO KEEP ON THE RIGHT SIDE OF HIM ...

FOR HE CAN GREATLY INFLUENCE YOUR CHANCES OF SUCCESS.

YOU WILL ALSO GET TO KNOW OF THE BEATERS

WHO COME FROM ALL WALKS OF LIFE . . .

AND DO IT AS MUCH FOR THE LOVE OF IT ,

AS FOR THE MONEY.

THE KEEPER WILL COMPLAIN HOW HARD IT IS TO GET GOOD BEATERS ,

AND THERE ARE ALWAYS EITHER TOO MANY,

OR TOO FEW.

THE MORE EXPERIENCED WILL ACT AS STOPS,

WHOSE JOB IS TO PREVENT THE BIRDS RUNNING OUT OF COVER.

FINALLY YOU WILL LEARN OF THE PICKER-UP,

WHO WILL WORK UNSEEN BEHIND THE GUNS ...

ACCOUNTING FOR THE BIRDS SHOT ,

WHETHER DEAD ,

OR THOSE UNFORTUNATE 'RUNNERS'.

TO COMPLETE YOUR EDUCATION, YOU MUST MASTER THE ETIQUETTE OF THE SHOOTING DAY.

BETWEEN DRIVES GUNS SHOULD BE BROKEN ,

OR SLEEVED .

BE SURE TO FIND OUT WHAT YOU ARE ALLOWED TO SHOOT AT

AND IDENTIFY YOUR TARGET ,
No. 4 SQUADRON
OPS. ROOM
PHEASANT MK. I
CODENAME : 'THE BIRD'
CEILING
RANGE
MAXSPEED
ARMAMENT
PAY ATTENTION CHAPS

BEFORE YOU SHOOT .

DID YOU EVER SEE A BIGGER PHEASANT ?

DO NOT ARGUE OVER SHARED BIRDS ,

AS IT CAN LEAD TO ILL-FEELING.

ALWAYS BE PREPARED TO OFFER LIFTS TO FELLOW GUNS,

AND IT IS ADVISABLE TO CONFINE YOURSELF TO THOSE GUNS

WHEN OFFERING YOUR FLASK.

LASTLY WHEN AN INVITATION IS RECEIVED,

ANSWER WITHOUT DELAY.

THE PHEASANT IS THE MOST POPULAR QUARRY ,

AND IS IN THE MAIN

SPECIALLY REARED,

OH...AND TWELVE DAUGHTERS !

AND ALTHOUGH EARLY IN THE SEASON

IT IS RELUCTANT TO LEAVE COVER . ,

LATER IN THE YEAR,

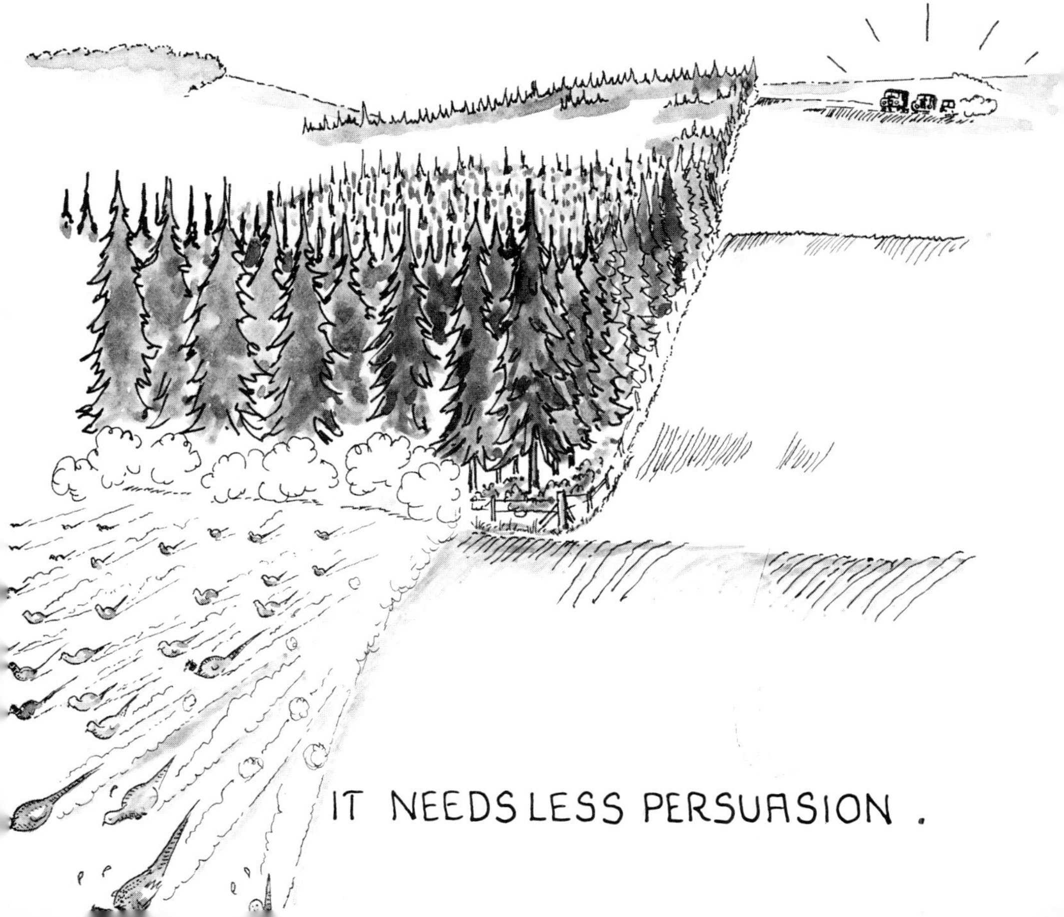

IT NEEDS LESS PERSUASION.

WHILE STEEP SLOPES ARE AN ADVANTAGE
MUMMY!
IN PRESENTING THE BIRDS OVER THE GUNS,

LOW GROUND CAN BE EXCITING . . .

GIVEN THE RIGHT CONDITIONS .

PARTRIDGES ARE LOVERS OF THE WIDE-OPEN SPACES

. . AND HAVE A TENDENCY TO TRAVEL IN COVEYS .

THE GROUSE APPEARS TO TRAVEL EVEN FASTER

AND LOWER THAN THE PARTRIDGE ,

BUT YOU WILL HAVE TO GO NORTH TO FIND THEM .

THE LARGER BLACKGROUSE IS SOMETIMES FOUND AS FAR SOUTH AS EXMOOR,

BUT IS NOT USUALLY SHOT THERE,

THEIR COUSIN THE PTARMIGAN, OR SNOW GROUSE,

IS ONLY FOUND ON THE MOUNTAIN-TOPS.

FINALLY THERE IS THE KING OF THE NORTHERN PINE FORESTS

IF YOU LISTEN CAREFULLY YOU WILL HEAR ITS CALL. . .

THE CAPERCAILLE OR GIANT GROUSE .

ASSUMING THAT YOU HAVE CHOSEN TO START

WITH THE EASIER PHEASANT,

YOU WILL NOW BE LOOKING FOR YOUR FIRST DAYS' SHOOTING.

UNLESS YOU ARE LUCKY ENOUGH TO HAVE A FRIEND THAT WILL INVITE YOU,

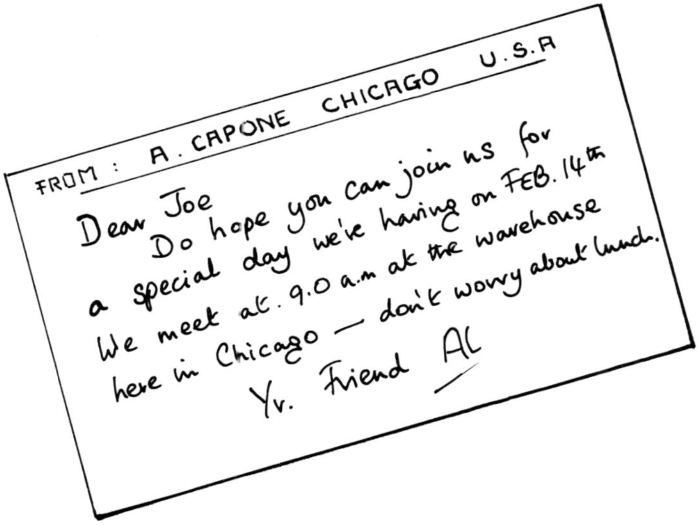
FROM : A. CAPONE CHICAGO U.S.A

Dear Joe
Do hope you can join us for
a special day we're having on FEB. 14th
We meet at. 9.0 a.m at the warehouse
here in Chicago — don't worry about lunch.
Yr. Friend AL

YOU CAN EITHER BUY A DAY FROM AN AGENT

OR ATTEMPT TO JOIN A SYNDICATE

IN A SYNDICATE, YOU WILL GET TO KNOW YOUR FELLOW-GUNS WELL

BUT ON LET DAYS YOU NEVER KNOW WHO YOU WILL BE SHOOTING NEXT TO

AND WHILE LET DAYS ARE RELATIVELY EASY TO OBTAIN ,

A GUN IN A GOOD SYNDICATE . . .

OFTEN DEPENDS ON DEAD MEN'S SHOES.

ON YOUR FIRST DAY MAKE YOURSELF KNOWN TO YOUR FELLOW - GUNS ,

BE MODEST ABOUT YOUR ACHIEVEMENTS,

AND BE READY TO GIVE CREDIT WHERE
IT IS DUE - WHATEVER THE CIRCUMSTANCES ..

REMEMBER TO STAND BEHIND YOUR PEG . . .

UNLESS OTHERWISE INSTRUCTED .

FIND OUT WHERE PEOPLE HAVE BEEN POSTED,

SO THAT YOU MAY SHOOT SAFELY .

AND AT THE END OF THE DAY ,

DO REMEMBER TO GIVE THE KEEPER A TIP ,

THEN, AT LAST YOU MAY RELAX,

HAPPY IN THE KNOWLEDGE

THAT YOU ARE NOW A RECOGNISED SHOT.

The Author is a Hampshire fish farmer whose Labrador Sam considers that the year consists of the months of AUG – JAN, and that the remaining months are a necessary evil to be endured until the next shooting season comes around. The Author's wife and two young daughters all ride, and he maintains that it was purely coincidence that his first book – "KINDLY ADJUST YOUR DRESSAGE" – was all about eventing.

Kindly Adjust Your Dressage.................................... £1.95
A Little Behind £2.95

The above books are available at your bookshop or newsagent, or can be ordered from the following address:
Hammer Trout Farm,
Liphook, Hants.

Please send cheque or postal order (no currency) and allow 45p for postage and packing for the first book plus 20p for the second book and 14p for each additional book ordered up to a maximum of £1.63 in U.K.

Customers in Eire and B.F.P.O. please allow 45p for the first book, 20p for the second book plus 14p per copy for the next seven books, thereafter 8p per book.

Overseas customers please allow 75p for postage and packing for the first book and 21p per copy for each additional book.